NUCLEAR ANNIHILATION AND HOW TO DRESS FOR IT

NUCLEAR ANNIHILATION AND HOW TO DRESS FOR IT

THOMAS BRENNAN

REGENT PRESS
Berkeley, California

Copyright © 2025 by Thomas Brennan

ISBN 13: 978-1-58790-715-9

ISBN 10: 1-58790-715-1

Library of Congress Catalog Number: 2025941025

Manufactured in the U.S.A.
REGENT PRESS
Berkeley, California
www.regentpress.net

I don't understand why men have to be buried in a suit and tie. It's not like they're going to see *Hamilton*.

Taylor Swift is so popular – when she clears her throat it's a hit.

I recently bought one of those tiny Smart cars but then I got to thinking. Should my leg weigh more than my car?

I never play craps. I won't play anything that sounds like a bowel movement.

I enjoy having company over. But then again I like getting hit in the eye with a tack hammer.

I stopped taking my new medication because of the side effects. For three weeks I thought I was Queen Victoria.

A bar is a place where everyone complains but nobody listens.

I had a yearly checkup the other day. I won't say my prostate is huge – but my doctor discovered the Lost City of Atlantis.

Your car is probably a clunker if valets pay *you* to park it.

I don't understand why so many hikers end up getting rescued. How hard is it to take a walk?

Vitamin supplements are for people too lazy to eat a grape.

I used to live in a town that was so strict – the nudist colony had a dress code.

I don't understand how Michael Myers managed to kill so many people in *Halloween*. How hard is it to outrun somebody who's walking?

I think they should allow performance enhancement drugs in the Olympics. I just want to see somebody run the mile in 8 seconds.

You get what you pay for. The other day I bought a DVD at a dollar store. The movie had commercials.

Spring is just another word for "Hey! Let's thaw out grandpa!"

**The trouble with wearing hearing aids is now
you get to hear bullshit a lot clearer.**

Halloween has really changed since I was a kid. I remember a time when everyone just went trick or treating. Today you pay a guy to chase you with a chainsaw.

I worry about my friend. He watches the Zapruder film to unwind.

My credit score is so low – the other day my cash was declined.

I can see why soccer is so popular. What's more exciting than a score of 0-0 after 4 hours?

A lot of people think the Royal family sits around all day and counts their jewelry. That's not true. They have other people count it for them.

I finally found the perfect cure for insomnia. I pay an accountant to call me up at one in the morning.

Apparently a lot of people get their news from TikTok. I wonder where they'll get their news from next- Cartoon Land?

How come Tarzan, Jane, and Cheetah all have names and yet they call their son Boy?

I hate it when a politician says there are way too my school shootings – like there's an acceptable amount?

Iowa is the only state where the leading cause of death is boredom.

I recently joined Procrastinators Anonymous.
I went to a meeting the other day – nobody showed up.

Question: How do you get a politician to say absolutely nothing?

Answer: Ask him a question.

I've had so much work done on my teeth – my dentist wrote me in his will.

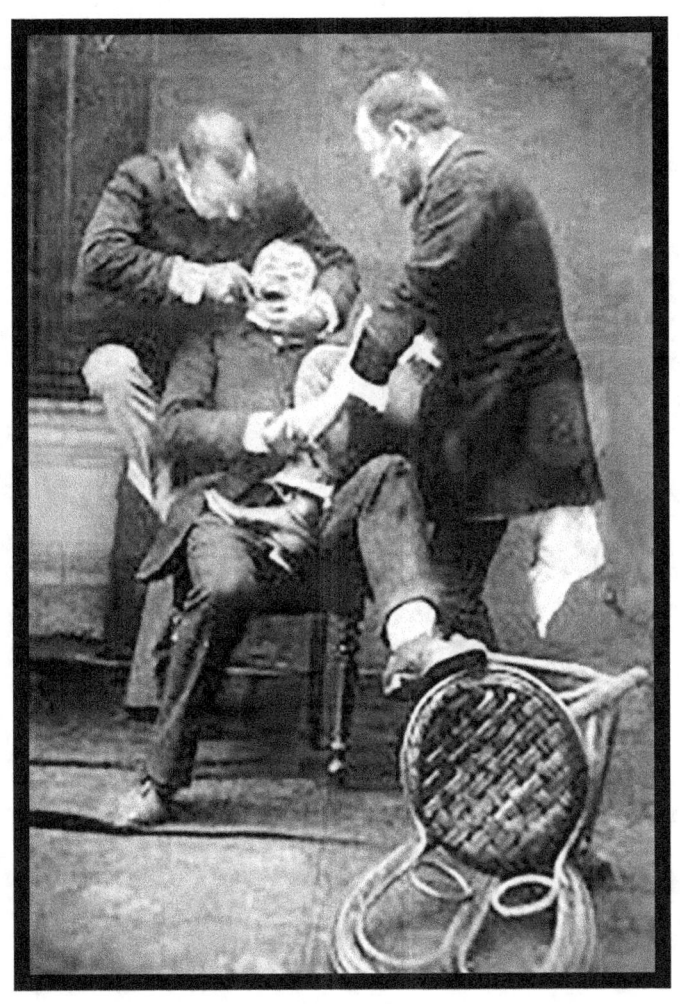

It sucks getting older. Every time I sneeze I have to change my underwear.

The economy is so bad – the other day I saw Elon Musk driving an Uber.

Stay away from restaurants if Kaopectate is a side.

My wife hates it when I snore. Especially when I'm driving.

It's impossible to square dance to bagpipes.

Did you ever eat a grape and pretend it's an eyeball?

The Ten Commandments never mentions slavery as a sin. Apparently it's okay to own people – but you better not screw your neighbor's wife.

What's up with everybody shopping in their pajamas? It's a store – not a sleepover.

I can tell I'm getting older. Ambulances are starting to follow me around.

**Quick note:
If you can't
pronounce it
you probably
can't afford it.**

I don't understand why people ask if you're okay when you're obviously not okay. You could fall down a flight of stairs and somebody will say "Are you okay? Can I get you something? Maybe a Fresca?"

There's something wrong with a society where children go to bed hungry yet we reward somebody for eating the most hot dogs.

We were so poor – my parents told me steam was a food group.

If you've ever walked a mile in someone else's shoes – you probably stole them.

Store managers have got to hire more cashiers. The other day I was in line for so long – the 100 Years War went by quicker.

I don't understand how scientists can discover distant galaxies but nobody can find Jimmy Hoffa.

Whatever happened to the good old days when the only time a religious figure wanted you on your knees was to pray?

Why do people say their alarm clock went *off* when in fact it went *on*?

Crime has gotten so out of control – the other day Dracula was reported missing.

I remember the time my dad warned me that masturbation can lead to blindness. I said to him, "Dad – I'm over here."

I recently attended a Hells Angels wedding. It was a wonderful ceremony. The bride and groom wore matching helmets.

I'm not saying my relatives never get along – but every year our Thanksgiving dinner turns into a crime scene.

If somebody offers you a breath mint – take it.

Any movie that features a cornfield never ends well.

The auto industry has finally come up with a solution to combat driverless car accidents. It's called a driver.

You can always tell a one-star restaurant. The sign outside says "Sorry – We're open."

The other day my Astrological sign said "Follow your dreams." That's what I like about horoscopes. They're so specific.

The economy is so bad exclusive restaurants no longer feature strolling violinists. Instead, a server comes up to your table and hums.

It sucks getting older. I used to bust a move but now I'm lucky if I don't break a hip.

The office is a place where dreams go to die.

The economy is so bad I saw a bouncer throwing people *into* the club.

I can't figure out how to use a universal remote. The other day I pushed a button – the TV didn't come on but my neighbor's car started.

Erectile Dysfunction is God's way of giving you the middle finger.

I went on a cruise that was so cheap – I weighed less *after* the trip.

I have the worst luck. I bet my life's savings on a horse they said couldn't lose. Not only did it finish last – they had to shoot the jockey.

I checked out this new deep discount store the other day. I could tell the food was old. The Wheaties box had a picture of Lou Gehrig.

Have you noticed the later it gets the more suspicious people look?

With great names like the Giants, the Pirates, the Tigers, and the Cubs, how come Boston named their baseball team after a pair of socks?

When you order soup and half a sandwich – who eats the other half?

My father was so frugal, every winter he'd set the thermostat to Gulag.

BOOKS I HIGHLY RECOMMEND

How Breast Implants Saved Our Marriage

Conga Lines You Should Avoid

How to Squeeze Fruit Without Appearing Anxious

Gravity – Is It Real?

How To Die Healthy

Amish Sex Secrets

How To Fake Your Own Death for Under a Buck

Christmas Songs for the Nervous

How to Make Hitchhiking a Career

Caligula: Behind the Laughter

PEOPLE I CAN DO WITHOUT

Guys who spend way too much time in wooded areas.

People who talk with their entire face.

Tesla owners who pull up to food banks.

Concert performers who make audiences sing along.

People who like their eggs runny.

Guys who respond to EVERYTHING with "That's what she said!"

Sports figures who wear a beard down to their nipples.

People whose eyes click when they blink.

Guys who call their wife "Mother."

Really bad ventriloquists.

People who celebrate Christmas 8 months early.

Families that wear matching pajamas.

Guys who lay on their couch all day and read fitness magazines.

People who post pictures of food on Instagram – like nobody has ever seen a pizza.

Anybody with a permanent grin.

Guys in their nineties who still run marathons.

People who think Kenny G is too edgy.

Expectant couples who say "We're pregnant."

People who hold a door open for me when I'm half a block away.

Guys with jet-black hair and a white beard.

Drivers who try to track me down after I've given them bad directions.

People who wish hurricanes were bigger.

Guys who keep hitching up their pants.

Anybody who catches me laughing to myself.

People who say "If I tell you
then I'll have to kill you."
And they mean it.

Identical twins
that dress alike.

People who whistle tunes
I can't make out.

Anybody who takes their
glasses off to make a point.

OXYMORONS

Passive aggressive

Semi-retired

Minor miracle

Small fortune

Light heavyweight

Semi-precious stones

Crash landing

Science fiction

Working vacation

Rubber cement

Undercover

Business ethics

Christian Scientist

Virtual reality

Historical fiction

Victimless crime

Political Science

Awfully good

Limited Lifetime Warranty

Water ice

Friendly fire

Loyal opposition

Foreign national

EUPHEMISMS

Layoffs ❖ *Merger*

Broke ❖ Liquidity problem

Heart attack ❖ Cardiac event

Loser ❖ Runner up

Old ❖ Mature

Racist ❖ Provocative

Prison ❖ Gated Community

Dump ❖ Recycling center

Invasion ❖ Special military operation

Gun control ❖ Gun safety

Barber ❖ Hair stylist

Drug use ❖ Self medication

Starvation ❖ Food insecurity

Homeless ❖ Unhoused

Bribe ❖ Donation

Desperate ❖ Highly motivated

Dieting ❖ Portion control

Exaggerating ❖ Aspirational

Strip mall ❖ Shopping destination

Disenfranchised ❖ Underserved

Over-crowded living quarters ❖ Multigenerational dwellings

Repair shop ❖ Maintenance center

Customer ❖ Guest

Gardener ❖ Landscape architect

Tornado ❖ Weather event

Employee theft ❖ Shrinkage

Lie ❖ Embellishment

Handyman ❖ Contractor

Rocket explosion ❖ Rapid disassembly

War ❖ Conflict

Plagiarism ❖ Duplicative language

Civilian casualties ❖ Collateral damage

Slow ❖ Deliberate

Coverup ❖ Credible narrative

Arrested ❖ Detained

Torture ❖ Interrogation

Out-of-style ❖ Vintage

Dead ❖ At peace

Flip-flop ❖ Evolve

Anal ❖ Purist

Discriminate ❖ Marginalize

Slaughterhouse ❖ Food preparation center

Out of control ❖ Fluid

Repulsive ❖ Complicated

Dilapidated ❖ Fixer-upper

Inconsistent ❖ Flexible

Car Wash ❖ Auto Spa

REDUNDANCIES

Free giveaway

Sit down

Overcoat

Aggravated assault

Eyewitness

Mutual alliance

Face mask

Cruise ship

Step ladder

Fresh start

Outer space

Corporate fraud

Multiple witnesses

Vast majority

New beginning

Over crowded

True fact

Active shooter

Breath mint

Deadly weapon

Unexpected surprise

FAMOUS HISTORICAL FIGURES

The following pages reflect some little-known facts concerning several intriguing and relevant figures.

George Washington was the colonists' Commander-In-Chief during America's fight for independence against the British. He is proudly regarded as the "Father of our Nation." Vice President John Adams was so jealous of George Washington – he used to secretly stretch Washington's knee socks so that they'd sag.

Napoleon Bonaparte is regarded as one of history's greatest generals.

In an effort to humiliate the French leader – the British claimed that Napoleon was so short he needed a step ladder to pet his cat.

Claiming to be a faith healer, Grigori Rasputin reportedly saved the life of Czar Nicholas's son Alexei who suffered from hemophilia. During the Russian revolution Rasputin tried smuggling the unpopular Czar and his family out of Russia by hiding them in his beard.

Former President Calvin Coolidge was so quiet and reserved he was actually pronounced dead at his Inaugural. After he left office, he grew a beard and sideburns and started a rhumba band in East Orange, New Jersey.

John Dillinger was one of the most notorious gangsters in the early 1930s. Dillinger was so cruel and sadistic – he once pistol whipped a server to death for spilling gravy on his spats.

First Lady Eleanor Roosevelt was instrumental in helping her husband Franklin pass legislation designed to improve the lives of America's disenfranchised. After leaving the White House she kept herself busy with gardening and adopting small men.

At one time Howard Hughes was one of the wealthiest business magnates in the entire world. Hughes was so eccentric – he liked to invite guests out on his private yacht and then sink it.

As one of the founding members of the Rolling Stones, Keith Richards remains a highly respected rock and roll icon.

On noticing Keith Richards wearing a bandana – Frank Sinatra took the rock star aside and said "Get yourself a parrot, an eyepatch, and go rob a ship."

The Job Interview

INTERVIEWER: Good morning, Mister Emmerich. As you know your parole officer was kind enough to allow us to interview you for employment at our firm. And as part of the job interview process I'm going to ask you to participate in a psychological evaluation. I'm going to say some words and after each word I want you to tell me the very first word that pops into your head. Are you ready?
EMMERICH: Yes.

INTERVIEWER: Wonderful. Now here is the first word. Happiness.
EMMERICH: Money.

INTERVIEWER: Farmer
EMMERICH: Daughter.

INTERVIEWER: School.
EMMERICH: Detention.

INTERVIEWER: Kittens.
EMMERICH: Lake.

INTERVIEWER: I'm sorry. You said lake?
EMMERICH: Yes.

INTERVIEWER: I see. Okay. Let's continue. Bank.
EMMERICH: Guards.

INTERVIEWER: Team.
EMMERICH: Gang.

INTERVIEWER: Fear.
EMMERICH: Police.

INTERVIEWER: Tool.
EMMERICH: Hacksaw.

INTERVIEWER: Fire.
EMMERICH: Arson.

INTERVIEWER: Okay. I'm going to stop you right here. You do understand that in order to pass this evaluation and thus gain employment at our firm you must be careful how you come across? I mean just between you and me your answers are somewhat – unorthodox.
EMMERICH: I'm sorry. I guess it's my nerves.

INTERVIEWER: I understand. Just take a deep breath. Relax. Let me know when you're ready to resume.
EMMERICH: I'm ready.

INTERVIEWER: Friend.
EMMERICH: Accomplice.

INTERVIEWER: Are you sure?
EMMERICH: Did I say something wrong?

INTERVIEWER: No. You're doing great.
EMMERICH: That's good to hear. Thank you.

INTERVIEWER: Enemies.
EMMERICH: Witnesses.

Interviewer: Candy.
Emmerich: School yard.

Interviewer: Shelter.
Emmerich: Hideout.

Interviewer: Children.
Emmerich: Hostages.

Interviewer: Okay. I think that just about wraps things up. Thank you so much for coming in Mr. Emmerich. We'll get in touch with you as soon as we make our decision. You have a nice day. Okay?
Emmerich: Wallet.

Interviewer: Well, you see, Mr. Emmerich. The evaluation is over. You can go home now. Have a nice day.
Emmerich: Jewelry.

Interviewer: Mr. Emmerich. We're done here.
Emmerich: Floor.

INTERVIEWER: I don't think you understand. You need to leave.
EMMERICH: I don't think *you* understand. This is a holdup. Get on the floor. (Robs the interviewer).

INTERVIEWER: But this is absurd! You'll never get away with it!
EMMERICH: I think I just did. Have a nice day!

www.ingramcontent.com/pod-product-compliance
Lightning Source LLC
Chambersburg PA
CBHW070113080526
44586CB00013B/1286